Psychology – memory flashback

Emotion, Sacrifice and Mercy

Fatema Miah

Part 1 Brain and Aggression types

page 3

Part 2 Memory, sacrifice and psychological pain

Page 16

Part 1

 Brain and aggression types.

Memory is the core part of human functioning, it's for the
memory human being are been able to function to get on with
daily activities, plan, organise and manage tasks, deliver services,
living well, and being able to identify, recognise the differ aspects,
time scale and enable by envisaging, and enrapture the visages of
articulate significance of individual visages differ identicalness,
and merely, the very memory is a very fragile aspect. The
memory what is on functioning normal enables beings to tasks,
usually, human being aren't even appreciative because it is being
taken for granted, for not being aware of its invaluable
importance. The same memory can deceive one and horribly
comes awful and painful, it plays contrary on ones motivation and
Intention, against ones will. It results to hurt, self hurt and nearest
and dearest ones get heart.

Psychology is the study of mind not the brain work. Let's add Brain
cortex and functionality, for little understanding about the brain
will help us to have understanding about the connection or
reaction of the two. The extraordinary success been possible with
persistence and perseverance of us human, by our thought
process, and pleasantly exercising functioning of our cortex. The

entire process of mechanism functions to create happiness. Parietal cortex, one of the four lobes of the brain "Processes sensory information that had to do with taste, temperature, and touch". The parietal lobe located in the middle between frontal (at the front) and Occipital and Temporal lobe (at the back). The lobes are bunched into one compacted wavy curled up bundle. Parietal cortex or lobe functions the sense, feeling, taste, perception, temperature and touch, and processes information within seconds. It sends the signals of emotional feelings of taste of like, dislike and pleasure, comfort and sensation of temperature of hot and cold though the bodily function. It is responsible for cognitive functioning. Endorphin: a substance in the brain that "attaches to the same cell receptors that morphine does". Endorphins substances are released when severe injury occurs, often eliminating all sensation of pain. Works same ways for the emotional severe injuries; at the after mouth of a rage or exhilaration. Physical exercise plays a vital part producing endorphins into the Parietal cortex.

 A substance medicinal-scientific named Myosin protein existence in the brain functioning drags the endorphins substance released through filament fibre on the Parietal cortex cell of the brain. The cognitive functioning is inclusive of reasoning, memory, Language, taking information and retaining knowledge. Because it is the process mechanism of information, language and knowledge, it also processes the output function of sharing information, making response to sense and talk. It is also directly connected to other factors such as mood and physical health. The hypothalamus is a small gland in the centre of brain, it is a "brain structure made up of distinct nuclei as well as less anatomically distinct areas". It is presents in all living being with segmented spinal Colum known as vertebrate with brain or nervous systems. Its function is to release hormones into blood cells and highly connected with central nervous system. From this gland hypothalamus hormones are produced through other parts of cells, released into blood through other cells, gets defused in process and released into the blood vascular system.

As well as it works to function the nervous system, and controls the various of hormones, the hypothalamus is also responsible for the metabolic processes. Hypothalamus gland is sitting in the tip of the spinal cord in the centre part of all brain cortex or lobes. It is connected to and functions all parts of the brain cells and the body cells. Feelings of all kind is the process of hypothalamus gland and it is vastly it is active functional in fully developed and grown up adults. This gland helps to control different cells and organs. The hormones from the hypothalamus govern physiologic functions such as temperature regulation, thirst, hunger, sleep, mood, sensual drive, and the release of other hormones within the body. This portion of the brain is small in size, it is involved in many necessary processes of the body including behavioural, autonomic (involuntary or unconscious), and endocrine functions, as well as metabolism it controls growth and development.

When it is in active functional state it releases the hormones as well as other hormones, the sensual pleasure-seeking feeling also enables the adults to convey the seeking message and drive into conduct appropriately and co-operatively. The hypothalamus glands functioning aids the acts of process; produce to sensation, release to pleasure and concludes with defuse. There is another small gland immediate above the hypothalamus at the top and centre section is Thalamus. From this gland nerve fibres projecting out to the cerebral cortex in all directions. The thalamus derives its blood supply from a number of arteries. Its functions are the relaying of sensory and motor signals to the cerebral cortex, and the regulation of consciousness, sleep, and alertness.

Via the spinothalamic cell it is connected to spinal cord that is a sensory pathway into the spinal cord. Vice-e versa, information gets passed to the thalamus about pain, temperature, itch and crude touch and pressure. The thalamus has multi-function also plays an important role in regulating states of sleep and wakefulness. The back cortex of the brain, is the occipital lobe located at the back, is one of the four major lobes of the cerebral cortex in the brain. The occipital lobe is the visual processing centre of the brain containing most of the functional region of the visual cortex. This lobe or cortex functions to work for the eye sight catches and process the signal and messages eye sight sending. Frontal lobe or the frontal cortex is one of the major cerebral cortex in the brain, and this is the largest cortex or lobe in the brain parts. This section of cortex is the fore brain and associated with reward, attention, short term memory, tasks planning and motivation. The frontal lobe or the fore part of brain plays a large role in voluntary movement and the primary motor cortex which regulates activities like walking. It functions the conscience like the ability to project future consequences resulting from current actions, the choice between good and bad actions.

Temporal lobe or the cortex is one of major lobe in brain located on the both side of the cerebral hemisphere. This lobe plays a key role in the formation of explicit long-term memory, its conduct high level of auditory process for example, works for the hearing and process of visual information. The cerebral functioning contributes to our happiness and simultaneously, dis-functioning or defect in any cells within those segments equally reason for misery or dissatisfaction in our lives.

I have Acquired Brain Injuries, the signs and symptoms are evident in my living, and attitudes. There are reports and records of witnessed and evident of Incurred head injuries on multiple of times in childhood and so repeated in adulthood. There are people involved in causing the injuries and further they are the same beings been attempting fullest to their capacities many ways to take advantage of my condition to further victimisation to suppress and control me.

Let's touch on nervous system : Instinctive Response to instantaneous. Work of nervous system is said to be, "heart responds faster than head" it's true in my sensory condition. The gut-reaction is very highly instantaneous, it results to trigger quickest heart palpitations, causes disturbing in instinctive response. The super-fast reaction of the guts and hearts quickest, super-speed reaction, the instinctive response doesn't leave enough time for mind to churn things over. Therefore, mind reacts as such that it cannot ponder on for a different possible or likely approach or interaction might be other than assimilation or expectation, rather in instantaneous reaction of hostility it triggers a feeling of being thrown off the guard, a kind of flashing

of panicking condition emerges and causes what is known as
'complex caveats'. Which is not only confusing to people,
(specially often in my case,) it causes block off effect though
momentarily, then again the moment is varied on the time scale
of hours, to days, weeks to years.

Psychology is study of mind, its formation is the conclusion of the
environment, and incidents as we are aware of. Memory divided into
two different segments of terms, of short and long term. The short
term memory is in functioning in daily routine based activities and in
constantly or regular exercised. The long term memory is what is put
to rest at the back of the mind and not in regular exercised or not
regular recall. The both short and long-term memory above brief
explanation is about in normal functional condition, as the known
norm, as happens to be the case or expected to be as such. Flashbacks
occurs from the segment of long term memory. There are differ
results from different condition or from abnormalities of incurred
damages by excess pressured distress from striken shocking
emotional pain, or direct injuries. Abnormalities condition Incurred
to both segments of short or long terms from above mentioned
damages. The impacts also can be vary, long or short term.

 Flashback with expressed feeling of emotion and sacrifice. The
memory Flashback is painful what brings up episodes of past occurred
incidents of both; unpleasant parts what causes dreadful paining,
displease feelings and distress. My personal experience and it's very
painful. The dear belonging parts of past causes missing feelings,
nostalgia and makes one to desire to go back. This feeling is very
distressing. It's not only that it isn't possible to go back, looking
back to time those moments were as such, I had no control on those
moments being a child I was helpless, where I couldn't do anything to
help the situation, or to do something differently on my behalf would

change anything, thinking back now neither should be remorse being not at fault, rather been in a suffering state myself. Overall, all together, it resulted to formed my psychological complication.

 Psychology and memory complexity; Instinctive Response to instantaneous. The maxim, "heart responds faster than head" it's true in my sensory condition. The heart reacts to the sense before the head can Interpret the sensory matter. The gut-reaction is very highly instantaneous, it triggers quickest heart palpitations, by reacting to its sensory mode, and causes disturbing in instinctive response. Instantly, the mind goes into sleep mode, result to withdraw by confusion, as the natural reaction it seeks to escape the complexity. Per to he complexity, the super-fast reaction of the guts and hearts accelerates, speeds up to fastest reaction.

The instinctive response therefore, it doesn't leave enough time for the mind to engage in the spontaneity to be able to churn the emerged unexpected incidents over. This is where the memory happens to be disengaged. Therefore, mind cannot ponder on for a different possible or likely approach or interaction might be. Rather in instantaneous reaction of hostility or feeling being thrown off the guard kind of panicking condition emerges and causes 'complex caveats". Which not only confuses us, (specially often in my case,) it causes block off effect though momentarily, then again the moment is varied on the time scale of hours, to days, weeks to years. In my case, there has been decades, to generation, a generation been passed from early childhood, passed over the youthood, to adulthood, through the childbearing age of motherhood, passing-through mid-age.

A sudden opening with a flashing memory flicking began, to adding on my chronic headache a year ago, in 2021. From 2020 a minder, lighter and shallow shadow been pasting through, almost like annoyance to my ignorance, I've been pushing out, wipe of to shake myself out of confusing distress. There people been playing not with positive input in it, rather contrary by their own misunderstanding and been unable to grasp the fact, per to misunderstanding were created by as usual to human assumptive nature makes them to dismissive to suit a certain crowd what usually blind them by negative dazzle.

While been extremely saddened from the explained occurrences, I was made to endure, what's I expressed in my books, Varied Expression and Disturbed psychology and evolution of Bangladeshis, and most people Involved in were too keen in brushing under the carpet by very little empathize, and unwilling to communicate to clarify, it hurt me differ and me cut through within. Simultaneously, the evils, and those mentioned in Disturbed psychology and evolution of Bangladeshis, are the culprits, known criminals and evils were let out free uncontrollable, resulted to many more including   innocent children been victimised (explained later in the next chapter).

Where, I have been voicing, and been facing pressure been applied on to oppress me by twists and play, manipulations, and feeding substances to caused Ill health to me. Memory flashes I have began experiencing. The nurture aspect of psychology comes up in it. There are world full of people come in with negative input of hurting and adding to hurt comes in. On the contrary, there are world full of people come in with positive input of caring and defensive in it. And some individuals fell in both ends. Those I cried with memory back, hurt me and been causing distress to me, played vast in making and spreading rumours, astonishing it is, one same fella, been risking his life in attempting of getting me. Suddenly, passed mid August, I am hit hard with a painful unexpected truth I could never imagine let alone to expect. My best the dearest, one nephew who's been playing best in my defence, been through shocking tumour remove head operation. It's killing me I dread my memory and nervous condition illness, for what I couldn't be there for him to take care of him.

Denial comes in with psychology and memory loss. Two types of Denial there are, one is, inability to accept the unpleasant truth, and one tries to hide under the cloud of hope, with faith. And another type of denial is the deliberate deny of ones aggressive and controlling nature. In Psychology and individuals' denial and there bias attitude often makes matters worse.   Let's have a touch on Psychology to express some individuals' bias attitudes. I studied psychology. Through observation I gather that Asian people are absolutely worse psychological disordered beings. As we are aware of from the basic knowledge and understanding of psychology that there are different effects and output of psychological factors. People are totally denials of worse category of psychological damaging factor. Faiths is hocked with psychology obviously.

A Muslim Imam and psychiatric spontaneously raised and mentioned white praising Islamic faith and he said here I quoted, as such: "I was a psychiatric for so many years and here in this region there are so many Muslims in this borough and only 2 % of Muslims are under psychiatric treatment, compare the percentage of other faith background groups, means Muslims are doing well and prayers helping". Yes, faith does help undeniable.

Well, being a devout Muslim I pray to please Allah the creator to fulfil my disciple obligatory duty, and I make (duas) whisper of seeking to Allah the Almighty to make things easy for us, Muslims and all creations, this is about well wishes. However, Allah the creator is unbiased and takes care of every living being in all situation and unconditionally. Knowing Allahs (Qadr) the planned destiny; there are certain procedures Allah has instructed and the best performers shall be rewarded, and harbouring faith (tawakkul) provides the strength (strength is my personal experience). We Muslims should be thankful in every condition because it could have been worse. However, taking oath on Islam and imposing being in the best form because of Islam it causes contradiction and raises questions. I believe it's abuse of Islam. Contrary, is it ego?

Whereas, Muslims are followers of Islam and Allah the creator promised the reward for the devotion and the good practises hereafter in the form of Jannah the heaven. This world is the place of test for believers, therefore life is not easy here for good people then knowingly why would Muslims comment as such?

 Has Islam become a source of Business banner that people try to entice by giving unwise and bad example?

 Is Islam used as a political weapon by democratically failed or incompetence being?

Surely it is the case that Islam is used as a weapon by majority Asian Muslim claimers in Asian countries and across the world, blindly ignoring the truth, rejecting the teaching of Islam and bending the rules according to individuals' and groups ill motive. Furthermore, Islam is also used for enticing Business profit by low quality products and services across the world. Here I bring the psychology linking to human behaviour. Psychology is the study of behaviour and mind and embracing all aspects of conscious and unconscious experience as well as thought. It is an academic discipline and an applied science which seeks to understand individuals and groups by establishing general principles and researching specific cases.

Referring back to the above Imam's comment, where he refused to address, overlooked, denied or being ignorant of true picture of the same group he referring to, that how vile, unpleasant, discord, and aggressive the individuals (most) are within the community. It is denial. It is matter of perception and cultural acceptances or norm that people are adopted to and they behave and expect certain behaviours for instance, ways of talk, body language and tone. The same exercised to different length/ depth which escalates to high or extreme level that leads to aggression. There are victims of aggressions and are oppressed.

There are different types of aggressions and psychology research findings show the different types of aggressions effect differently. Also different factors do influence aggressions, thus, aggression in all form is a negative impact for society and individuals. In plain and simple term, who enjoys bullying? No one!

There is a certain effect of such nature to other individuals. Such effects are rather unpleasant and damaging because it is either influencing the same aggressive mannerisms by discouraging pleasant soft nature or directly attacking on softer nature individuals. Hostile, Big voice and forceful talk of narrow minded assumption and intimidation are the signs of aggression. The victims of the aggression are the sufferers not the aggressors often, sometime also some are. Now, should I be fearful of truth? In Asian countries it is open out before the world the aggressive outlet is in evident. The same nature applied by Majority Asian people effecting others. It is as a norm. The Aggressive natured are in control and are controlling the communities, households, work places, and ever school gates standing places are attacked and gets galloped by some individuals (of my experience).

Several categorical types of aggression there are and they are Affecting Aggression, Impulsive Aggression, Instrumental Aggression and Predatory Aggression. Interestingly, researchers have suggested that individual who engage in affective aggression, defined as aggression that is unplanned and uncontrolled, tend to have lower IQs than people who display predatory aggression. Predatory aggression is defined as aggression that is controlled, planned and goal-oriented.

Instrumental aggression, also known as predatory aggression, is marked by behaviours that are intended to achieve a larger goal. Instrumental aggression is often carefully planned and usually exists as a means to an end.

Impulsive aggression, also known as affective aggression, is characterized by strong emotions, usually anger. This form of aggression is not planned and often takes place in the heat of the moment. When another car cuts you off in traffic and you begin yelling and berating the other driver, you are experiencing impulsive aggression.

Certainly, Muslim people are not immune to any of above aggressive categories in fact majority are to the extreme end of all and in denial.

Part 2

The memory, sacrifice and psychological pain.

Patches of dark time period has been passed through been
unknown, or left with big gap in the memory lane. Without those

gap patches, there has been horrendous painful full of moments, almost constantly enforced to under go, one been trying to leave with pain, by compromise, by taken into consideration, by giving into in comparison and by forgiving. Though, the highest degree of sacrifice making and nurturing mercy with dreadful tremendous endurance of highest killing pain by nearest and dearest ones attacks of deliberate plotted, constant conspiracy and taking pity of mercy with hypocritical lies, what goes buried into unconscious mind.

Eventually, hits hardest at the awakening to long and deep buried hard paining memory. Memory pain is hardest and sharpest pain. Feeling worse painful moments of being on the like killing moment, when by waking someone up by hard shaking, loudest sounding with gathering up everyone causing loudest bang and to go silent on the woken shocking moment. Suddenly, came to know mid August 2022, a dearest nephew gone through head operations. The slitting concern what been passing through about him, what been override for his bravery and for his assertive stance, came back to hit hard with pain, that the bravery bore down with stress and has weighted him down to resulted to such critical condition to his dear health. I over and again come to face my failure, that I failed often, on how to differ? Could I have deter the result at some point? Thinking back about when I wrote my book Ache in my heart.

Over the past few years of COVID-19 break out, and my memory flashing began, when it was a stressful time on the earth. The time indeed was a painful period, emerged as a shock; for pandemic virus spreading it comes with fear of health, shortages of essentials, and imposed with restrictive lockdown and new mandates. Fear of deaths and loss of loved ones, stress over health of self and nearest ones, and sudden income shortages, became the biggest danger. I began to suffer memory flashing back pain. It is saddened, people had to bear loss of loved ones and fought suffering COVID viruses. Its further, saddening that during COVID-19 lockdown period there weren't much of support to emotional suffering beings, neither enough care was on offer as usual for people to overcome their sudden unexpected departs. COVID19, is a landmark.

For the death departs pain, there is a solace, by faith. There is a bereavement service system, for comforting, to help people to be able to cope with departing pain. Although it's not so easy though, easier to take on with pain and sorrow, we manage to accept, its naturally accepted as Norn. May be because faith the believe of that the Angel comfort relatives, loved ones with magic rubbing stone onto the chest. Faith works for the believe of deeds and heaven, there is an assurance of they shall be resting in peace by good deeds of charity and worshipping, and after all, with the belief of the hereafter of Eternal Heaven. It's sorrowful though out of ones grip.

Whereas, the living attachment-detachments pains are severe painfully killing pain kind, because there is the living beings are involved in. It's worse when they are suffering too. The pain is even worse when you awake to know they were suffering all along. Sacrifices is a sharper cutting double edge knife on ones functional heart, weakest the heart it falls in the compelling intrigued game to be chopped under the sacrifice knife. When giving sacrifices, one doesn't realise it's cost of burden and consequences. Where the sacrifice is to giving into evils demands, for exchange of self ruining, pain taking, helplessly, on the spot giving in. Or there also sacrifice is for Compassion. For the compassion there is a little hope of exchange, to be bringing of betterment of if not for compassionate ones self at least for the one you doing it for, to bring a positivity out of negativity. This is in the aware condition, in consideration scenario. More or less, in this case, some positive aspects of emergence of positive outcome happens to be as the result. For reassurance (or for self deception).

In the other scene, being compelled by nature, naturally, when one is characteristically, compassionate and sacrificing natured for being too soft hearted, and sacrifice for weaknesses, being under evil pressure or under threats being helplessly burdensome there it often results to prolong, nagging, dragging pain suffering. The scenario or the situation forms as such that often, or eventually, re-emerges come back to staring at your face before your eyes, hit hard back flat on your face. The worse pain is to realise sacrifices been such a waste and there has been on going chronic sufferings occurred, and many been through endurance. Verily, there faults, blames, accusations, offends and allegations do mounts up, pushed up with levelling rightly and wrongly, or in mixed up per to confusion, bias, envy and vengefulness and for motive of personal and political agenda. After all, victim is victim one is the simple, naive innocent be the worse effected. Per to the phenomenally repeated history it is as usual. Irony also inevitable, like systematic norm is found not been gone amiss.

I have endured all forms of above expressed and experienced living hell, after awaken, I am pushed face on, to trace back on the tread line and shaking with paining. From head injury memory shifts headaches, pain striking memory flashes, to coming back flashbacks, kills me. Different fantasy like world appears in picture. I am far too delicate, too weak, I can't cope with memory its paining severely.   At the Covid-19, post- vaccination stage era, I am awakening to some pain striking memory cliffs. There were some missing links of memory gaps over the past 3 decades. The period of 3 decades what's meant to be my fullest education, experiences and academic, growing to grown up age stages, of youth -single to married-hood, and motherhood to carrying and conveying following generation through unknown voyage into like galaxy terrestrial. It's a sharp jolt awakening.

I been often have seek death, before the last past two decades, in the earlier 1st of the 3 decades, though, I never got it. Even my severe suffering body kicked off cancer, of the initial stage cell, it didn't develop to further stage, what was on international news two decades ago, and this was In the 2nd of 3 decades. I was pleased with God, I thanked God repeatedly for such miracle because I had two 2 infants. I still do appreciate this one particular miracle for sake of my two loving sons. Death went passed me many times during, before and after that too. I do question, on those other incidents why I didn't die? I endured, like spiral in storms wrap, swung across from coast to coast by drag across rubbing and whacking, through the rocky hills. There remained envy of known and unknown beings, with their zeal for no apparent reason, when I had no sense of their existence, neither any I harboured any enmity towards them, nor they let alone to justify thy can't even explain a reason for their tortures.

From an exchange of expression on someone's commemorational posts, my past weeks to months old pondering and awakening paining memory flashes led to starting on the such sobbing, like "an epic description of all our sorrows" from their moan over death of loved ones. I have Living chronic pain way huge and deep, high worse and harder then those over death moans. The attach-detach, pain is extremely severe. I am extremely anxious that my severity of pain feeling does not anyhow hint a sense of me being insensitive to their pain and ignorantly making it littler to my cry. I didn't die, with tremendous amount of endurances, like hitting between stones and rocks, storming up to thrown down, and I was further tested with two full term pregnancies to the final stage of having new-borns. Furthermore, they were put to pain striking trials and endurance. And, where it comes to my total-break down. On awakening from this prolonged shutting, further emergences of glim of shocking paining flask-backs taking place. In them emerging the faces with occurrences those were lost from my memory board. And there appears to be attach-detach paining. My question is why the angels don't come to solace on living attach-detach pain?

I do not like issues to be tenderised. In my Paining, male are in the scenes fighting over me causing me horrendous sufferings and in the scenes there were women behind, at the core, and in between each and every time fuelling and meddling up. Often ridiculous question people ask and compel you to engage in responding. Should women rule to world a question came up. With presumption of there will peace and no wars if women rule the world. My addition is women have ruled and it was worse devastating for women. More women or always it was were tortured, suffered and abused for power by women and men of women, and men those wants women, and of course by the envy men. Since this tenderised question been asked, I continued, may I answer with, per to traditionalised phenomenality based on the physical strength ability and balance capacitation of male passion its been better under male ruling. Male envy towards women is a very ugly painful mess, where women's envy towards men is distressing calamity.

Sub question to the question goes on, male ruling versus female ruling preferences is asked and the answer depends on what is expected as on the point of the very questioning in terms of population increase or decrease. The both factors of a) in birth, b) in massacre, to be reflected upon, to be taken on board to bring it to the conclusion. Then again, furthermore question arises what would they like to be done with men? Is the biggest factor here we need to know for the answer. There has been wars under women ruling too and worse of decision led to made by bad actions of men. Some men are prone to extremism under women's direction or manipulation and there are others are good at playing dictation. It's not all about gender play, it's power play and collaboration.

Previously, I wrote about how women are abused in work sectors in Asia and Africa by gender politicise. Exploitations are politicised and made to be normalised where other women are in the scenes too taking things for granted. Pain causing and compelling to endurance is not just a gender game. A chapter included in my book Varied Expressions. And in the same book another chapter I added about male tantrum, about domination in the past millennium in faith formation with women's destiny affirmed for example of St John and At Paul. Women's pain bearing made to be norm. Then again men decided to alter the system to no faith and to legalised Homosexually as an option, is there no abuse and pain?. What's happening to men and women co-existing, on shared decision-making?

Human beings are awkward creature like an strange painting of mere psychology creating. The evils ones are not in large number though they do make impact of deep and vast and their perpetration damages their victims, to irrecurable, turn to unchangeable and causes continues suffering. The people do support the perpetrators throughout, by not retaliation, not punishing, and by going to silent by denial, deliberate lie. Suffering, and victimisation continues. From there on opens up, irony, channels of further perpetrations to suffering victimisations.

I reiterated again and wrote this year in 2022, let's stop what is Crime and Haram, to prevent suffering and to protect Islam from being humiliated. Muslims are worse abused by Muslims! I made urge let's please step up to speak out loud for good against bad, to support, protect and guide children and adolescents, against those evils created systematically haram made into conventional by twisting to distortion. This continued while I have been vocalising throughout, wrote my book Disturbed psychology and evolution of Bangladeshis, the same perpetrators continued, under the same supporters through the same manipulators, I repeatedly mentioned and shouting about.

Muslim women in Burqa are sexual abusers, maniac and sickening criminals, in UK. Other those wear Burqa and Niqab know this must speak up and openly punish those few evil ones for sake of Islam, Quran and Halal, for Hudud and Al-Quran. If they don't they are cursed, their death won't be with (Iman) faith as it's I studied in Quran, and as the result their child's will be misguided victims. They same perpetrators victimised children. There is o e resulted to a 13 year old boy been abused and they made him a father of a baby girl. I love the child the 13 year old boy although I didn't know him, Gods bleessings and (my Duas) with him, I came to know who he is now, he is a pure and gold. The 13years old tries to speak to me on a number of occasions. I couldn't understand him for forceful emotion in his teenage voice. After underdoing who he is I want to speak him, I am trying to talk him since July 2022.

Muslim people and certainly Bangladeshi people   must set up example by punishing Shopna Akter in public through media. Evil Shopna Akter and (her misled manipulating daughter Bushra) are the culprits. In my book Disturbed psychology and evolution of Bangladeshis I wrote about Shopna Akter, wife of Jalal Uddin, Dagenham, London. I offered help for Bushra, through those people Bushra came to their house, cried on Eid day, for she cried that she wants to become good and she said that she gave birth to a baby and breastfeeding the baby, (and the father of the baby girl is a child Nusrath told me on the phone), Bushra wanted me to forgive her. I avoided the topic because I couldn't recognise Bashra, I don't like to talk on those kind of topics of conversation unless I am dealing with the case.   Now know this is linking to my book and they are the perpetrators. There is a linking lots in the whole chain, are involved in it those caused me horrendous sufferings.

The evil mother of Bushra must be punished in public and Bushra spoke truth about her mother and these people began to oppress Bushra. I want him to live his teenage years as he likes to like others teenagers do. Muslims allowed further damages by being playful, watching evil doing evil acts, and brought to this further unpleasant result. I offered that want to help the baby girl too. No more twists, no more distortion and falsification, to be allowed, no more cannot be brushing under carpet to hurt many others. Muslims must stand up to make it a lesson. To teach many , what is forbidden is not good. This same Shopna Akter mother of Bushra (wife and daughter of Jalal Uddin) they hypnotise people to unwell. They carry drug substance with them and drug people.

In my book Promptings and iterations on Amazon, I have shared the story of a saint Nijam Uddin Auliya. How he became a saint from an ordinary looter bandit. The story is such; when a man dug up a new grave and began to rape the copse, the bandit couldn't tolerate such and attacked and killed that evil man to prevent such immoral act. Adolescents delicate age state, when they are shoot up to reached suddenly a critical state of puberty, versus facing society norm and under the shadow of shyness, together there they having the challenging strength, bravery on worldly matters, where faith and social system is essential factor, if they are presented with such convulsed preaching certainly will misguide them, provokes a counter challenge in them, they can be misled easily.

This preacher Ubaid Ullah Amini spoke during hajj in one of the journey in coach in 2018 in Makkah about another story of man raped a copse after been buried of. Such Muslims tale which happened in Madina. The preacher narrated the tale as such and it was nothing but annoying. This man fancied this woman, she was married to another man. One day when she dies her family Husband, sons and other relatives buries her and went home. This man came to and dug up the grave and had sex with the copse. This must be noted; had sex with the copse. It's a copse and he had sex? Not rape. The copse spoke up after that said you did this to me now, how do I go and show my face to God as such? Note again, a copse, dead, buried, let alone woman it's dead body, she just because she is a woman how she is going to show her face to God? And what is God about? What message do they give to people to understand what? If anyone question on this moral of story they will be accused of disrespect to Islam and Allah the God. Is Allah a women hater?   My answer is no.

 Preachers preach on topic Zina the adultery, and women are blamed as the usual are as norm. Women of Asian were accustomed to preachers blames and to be faking shamed. Shame or shy was made into another sickening psychological factor. It was fake because it was hypocritical, women acted certain way as such as, they two-faced in their acts, and speech towards others and denial to their husbands, father's and preachers. (Eventually, in UK in past 10-15 years, UK Muslim sons standing up to correcting their mothers by catching them, for sake of their understanding of topic bias and for sake of correct Islam). Those preachers made women into culture of faking shy as to "doth protests too much" kind, unnecessarily. Where preachers were poisoning the society that the bad and dangerous men been taking advantage of faith preaching against women, women were put to danger, on the parallel there women suffered pain caused by other women for the ill mind-set, hate and jealousy. They all use phrase it as for sake of Islam. Clearly, Islam has been abused.

Bangladeshi ethnic people get eager to talk about, to gossip on any matter, they know the truth, they aren't Interested because once things are cleared up, when evils and bad ones are shown clearly, it's not to their like anymore, they only want to abuse by gossips. They in fact been supporting evil Shopna Akter. Bangladeshi group is the Worse category they are most of then into restaurant, grocery or media they use word media they are Involved. The Bangla channels ran by worse lowest of disqualify manned beings. They cry others discriminate Bangladeshis, false again because they are now not only worse beings in the lowest category they are dangerous too. Truth among them they are enduring also each others maliciousness. Totally, they have ruined Bangladesh, allowed Bangladesh to be ruined, and absolutely disgraced the ethnic category.

 The men of that ethnic group are worse abused by their women. The some of the same abused men go around talking false, bias giving in fact forcing opinion on others, causing damages and suffering to others. Some take suffering in silent. There are men those were force to be unwanted husband, deceived /abused / their sexual vulnerability/youthfulness been blackmailed / abused to be father, are made to sex slaves, enslaved under husband hood, left totally unloved, emotionally bitten up, unsatisfied, stress, to depression. From their vulnerability or silent treatment there on, they seem to be led on to this new turning to a group of new generation. They remained in darkness, carrying on their back, without noticing getting stubbing on their backs. Wives having partners. Men those husband to unwanted marriage of dislike in open used UK's right of phrase of partner. They been in the scene of those wives of enslaved husbands.

 I remained totally remote of that society, I knew nothing for my memory loss on chapter I didn't let open, nearly 40 years of flashing pain constantly I suffered. About the teenage father boy, I ignored the boy in May 16th, he called me mum and I took it as a joke because I couldn't understand the raised conversation . My prayers for him for his gestures and thoughts. I am further victimised by their enemies also, it has been going on for decades. Plotted conspiracy and further attacks deceptively been carried on. And in it, there were same being to the root and always, since my childhood. They also by manipulation though twisted lies pulled others being into their talking, though, their lies and manipulation not only proven false also opened up with other socking chapters of those being they pulled in been stubbing on their backs too, been on going for a long while.

 The boy called me mum again and again, and on the 16th May people been playing with his emotion and childish approach and innocent manner. How was I supposed to help it otherwise when I couldn't grasp what was going on? Then again on the 17th of July he gave me some messages, clicked to me later on , days later in fact. On those both days he took pics my pictures. I refused contact exchange because I didn't know it was him in May. Blessings to him for his such passionate , loving, affection. JazakAllah, Gods Blessings on him. Some other lads, young men rushed him out of the way on the 17th , I was left wondering what been going on. I am concerned for the him and his father, it's a different matter. I've been giving messages through those people again and again, have they been conveying the messages, I wondered, surely not, I understood.

My sons wanted to meet him the teenage boy to accept him as their little brother since he's seeking for mother's love from me. I messaged for him to come forward without hesitation. I knew he has been under oppressive control I noticed, though by whom, I can't understand his exact state, and what has been happening . There are people playing ill politics of manipulation. I couldn't recognise him every time he came to me because I get black out and then this blankness in head. There is no biological connection to me, it's their psychological nurturing attachment they have been harbour, carried on, I wasn't aware of till May, June, from then on it was flashing on, off then in July it became more apparent to me.

Since he told me he's a father of a baby girl, have made special cultural little traditional thing for your baby daughter and my love to shower on them all. It is affection he's seeking. In my understanding gathering of talks, that there are people playing not so positive. I am sad feel bad for the teenage boy, I react upset from his approach because he has sad feelings of real upsetting that he's been longing to get mum's love, although I am not guilty, not faulty neither have any connection, I am very saddening shamefully sad, in his approach I sense his painful longing expression of his unloved expectations of motherly affection from me, it is tantrum kind, straight hard it was in March, in April and in July. In July, being straight and kind of clingy and attached kind of feelings he had, I appreciate it and empathize to it. Though in May he was very well balanced despite being under pressure, was suppressed, I felt for him that he wasn't treated well. I sensed something is going on not so right. I didn't recognise him though he said a lot in those moments, neither I knew him, he added he doesn't get a hug. A teenage boy barely age 13 been abused, exploited, he doesn't get hug from female motherly relatives, for example of from his 1st line aunties.

I became too stressed and not known what can I do, since both father and son are not talking straight. The boy is a child and he tried his best, Weldon. All he needed is him to tell me who he is, an Introduction would have helped us. These women are cruel, evil, insensitive, carless and hurtful and they have been controlling with power. Who give them the authority and right to power exercise in the name of culture, or community? The abusers, they abuse cause suffering to many. Worse happens to them though, they don't feel the effect on them because they don't have sense of good things like peace and tranquillity. Other beings near them end up carrying the burden of their effects too. They cause suffering and compel people at the same time to carry their burden.

I, feeling very distress that after I knowing some things and I had so much memory back flashes. Here, I have to end the chapter with the blank pages again because after knowing the shadow wasn't just a mere shadow it is the real being, with many other loving beings in the tale, (they're related among themselves) touched my heart to a bit deep in with the sweetness, though, being remote and distance.   (The real beings, is it ego or enmity I fail to understand?) I leave it blank, may be time will, in the future decades to century later,   the blank will be filled to connect the chapters up. Will it not be manipulated again to distortion by deliberate manipulation of twists?) Too many people playing with false, to distort this extraordinary truth what's been constantly hit by evils, destiny, time and circumstances over and again.

I must say that some people love to keep crying and running, how can I help them? They love blaming, for example, to blame me like innocent because it's easy for blame game. Or they blame destiny. It is self-pity and they adapt to this attitude, they made it as a custom. Still they trying same old ways, they trust wrong crowd, hitting in the dark. There these father and son, been jumping up at me, (on my nerve because of peoples reactions, you see), going around to Bengali functions and social places, son calling me mum it's fine and sweet though it wasn't clear to me. I wasn't aware of them. Now, when I have gathered some understanding, by hard pushing through my injured head, to connect to memory, and being compelled to my heart, my sons want to meet teenage boy to accept him as their little brother, for what the boy seemingly wants, though, now both the father and son took depart, may be they aren't interested in it anymore, found their source of comfort somewhere else? It's fine to me and my sons. It's not that they don't get the message at all.

Of course there is no biological connection to me, it's their
psychological nurturing attachment they have been harbouring,
carried on, clang on to, I wasn't aware of till recently, in May, June
it was flashing on, off then in July it became more apparent to me.
It shocked me to almost death painting. The teenage boy calls me
his mum ok and sweet. My sons agreed to accept him. I didn't give
birth to him neither biological relationship between us. I didn't
know he was born, till now. I wasn't in Bangladesh. I didn't give
birth in Bangladesh at all. I only carried two matriculated well
Measured planned pregnancies in UK both babies born in UK.
My holiday to Bangladesh with my sons was for a week only in
December 2007. The teenage by was born in Bangladesh he's
telling people in Asian shops making me a liar to bad minded,
confusing kind of minded people, it's getting dangerous for me.
Further, he has a baby girl, when himself being a child, he is a
father by been abused, his tale is not only damaging me also
scaring my angel like, academic focused sons, pure ethical and
values respective with high moral principled lads my sons are.

After all, we love the teenage boy father of the baby girl. My sons
won't even question him being a parent, he is fine as his exists.
Without us talking among us matter gets unpleasant and
misleading , I cannot get people to comply to come up to a co-
operative understanding/acknowledgement to make it socially
pleasant. Do we he need a narration ? Telling ones place of birth
to people is unnecessary. By the way it falls in confidential
category. By the way, when boy's father spoke to me, in Feb 20th
he was under bad group of Bengali peoples bad play / control. It
was strange and shocking to me their approach was, I didn't get

the message right for I have been unwilling to communicate, I've been dismissive I can admit, (though my block knock off effects Triggered off). It was all of sudden, totally out of blue, unexpectedly, he by plan with many others came before me. Took me by shocked, knocked off to upsetting for deep buried emotion been dug up suddenly, brought to the surface.

Their approach in places, among many others, seemingly not making true positive portray. Bad people take bad end of anything and by everything they fault others, one they make faulty for saying something, make them wrong for not saying something they want and then again by abusing it they fault one said it after their wrong doings and sayings. These women, make this teenage boy father carrying his baby girl in his arms, walking in shopping malls, spreading the message of he's being a father of the baby and poi to g at me being mother of the father of the baby girl, when I don't know the lad, the lad who calls me mum. I being a mother of my grown up lads, I do not shy away being called mum by lads, in fact I take it with a pride, therefore, I do not dismissive nor argue.

I coming up with awakening from memory loss. I recall, the teenage boy's father suffered pain of loosing me, (not having me) since youth- hood, he nurtured desire to have me and he gets happy with his own assumptive wish he harbour in himself, holding me in his heart as his closes one, in his own thoughts. From his. 1st puberty age, he began to force his desire upon me, he was dying ad been harsh on me, asserting he is in love with me and I must only love him back. I was a child, and I was too young to respond to his such feelings, Y he himself exclaimed before me in the present of those people he came with. Where, he is a stranger man to me when even I face him. I however, have an automatical reaction of his feeling that I feel hurt, deep in my heart, I am unaware of and therefore, do not know how to handle it or to cope with the pain that's triggers off. I came to know his name is Anhar Ahmed Sabu is his nick name, he knows everything about me and my family members even more than I know about my family members.

This above mentioned Shopna Akter married her cousin by forcing him against his will and came to UK by marriage. The cousin husband of her, he refused her and this marriage and he refused to bring her to UK. One child of Shopna Akter, didn't match his DNA, and been agreed with prove that the daughter was result of her sickening sex. Shopna Akter abuses her two daughters all different ways.   The Cousin husband, of Shopna Akter, Mr Jalal Uddin wanted to marry me when I was a teenager. I refused him. In rage, and for he could accept the refusal, he chasing me, caused accidents and injured me on few occasions, no wonder why I am dreadfully scared of him, passing by me, I can't even see him for my deadly frightening feeling, my psyche sense him passing by me and I get frightened to automatically, screaming comes out with senseless blocked off effect. Despite I refused to marry him, still he refused her and he has been causing thunder-like destruction behind me, attempted all kind of harassing distress on me.

Shopna Akter is the one in my book Disturbed psychology and evolution of Bangladeshis. It is her, she made her daughter Bushra to sexually abuse that teenage child boy and Bushra is the mother

of the baby girl. They both mum and daughter attacked on me
August last year, 23 and 24 August 2021 in 126 Longmore Road
B90 UK.

There are many members of Bangladeshi ethnic people involved
in this web. Many are culprits in adding to my pain, causing my
pain, oppressing truth, falsification and in attempting to cause my
destruction. In interconnection among themselves. I have
touched, in Disturbed psychology and evolution of Bangladeshis. I
have to write more in different books narrowing down by subject
by breaking down explaining every events.